WINTER SPORTS

HOCKEY

Greg Siemasz

Raintree

Chicago, Illinois

© 2014 Raintree
an imprint of Capstone Global Library, LLC
Chicago, Illinois

To contact Capstone Global Library, please
call 800-747-4992, or visit our web site,
www.capstonepub.com

Edited by Adam Miller, Nancy Dickmann,
and John-Paul Wilkins
Designed by Richard Parker and Ken Vail Graphic
Design
Picture research by Elizabeth Alexander
Originated by Capstone Global Library Ltd
Production by Vicki Fitzgerald
Printed in the United States of America in
North Mankato, Minnesota

122013
007944RP

**Library of Congress Cataloging-in-Publication
Data**
Siemasz, Greg.
  Hockey / Greg Siemasz.—1st ed.
    p. cm.—(Winter sports)
  Includes bibliographical references and index.
  ISBN 978-1-4109-5451-0 (hb)—ISBN 978-1-4109-
5457-2 (pb) 1. Hockey—Juvenile literature. I.
Title.

GV847.25.S48 2013
796.962—dc23   2012042736

Acknowledgments
We would like to thank the following for
permission to reproduce photographs: Alamy pp.
9 (© Eileen Langsley Olympic Images), 15 (© RIA
Novosti), 18 (© MARKA), 24 (© Robert McGouey),
34 (© Stefan Sollfors), 35 (© Mark Spowart), 38 (©
Keith Hamilton/Southcreek/ZUMAPRESS. Com);
Corbis pp. 6 (© Sampics), 7, 13 (© Bettmann),
25 (© Christopher Morris), 26 (© Saed Hindash/
Star Ledger), 28 (© Andrew Dieb/NewSport), 37
(© PCN); Gerry Thomas/NHLI via Getty Images
p. 27; Getty Images pp. 4 (John Kelly), 5 (Robert
Riger), 8 (Roger Viollet Collection), 10 (Pictorial
Parade/Archive Photos), 12, 14, 23 (B Bennett), 20
(Bruce Bennett), 21 (Martin Rose/Bongarts), 22
top (George Silk/Time & Life Pictures), 29 (Claus
Andersen), 30 (Jonathan Daniel), 32 (Melchior
DiGiacomo), 33 (Jim McIsaac), 36 (Frederick
Breedon), 39 left (Hannah Foslien), 39 right
(Ronald C. Modra/Sports Imagery); Shutterstock
pp. imprint page (© Studio Kwadrat), 10 (©
iofoto), 16 (© Aspen Photo), 17 (© Alhovik), 19
(© PhotoStock10), 21 (© TRINACRIA PHOTO), 22
bottom (© Michael Pettigrew), 31 (© katatonia82),
33 (© MariusdeGraf), 40 (© Lorraine Swanson), 45
(© Shell114), 47 (© Flashon Studio); SuperStock
pp. 11 (Michael Interisano / Design Pics), 41
(Photononstop).

Design features reproduced with permission
of Shutterstock (© Nicemonkey, © Apostrophe,
© Lonely, © Nik Merkulov, © Designer things,
© Nik Merkulov, © design07, © AlexTois, © siart,
© Vaclav Volrab, © photographer2222).

Cover photo of a hockey player going for the puck
reproduced with permission of Corbis (© Duomo).

CONTENTS

Some words are shown in bold, **like this**. You can find out what they mean by looking in the glossary.

MIRACLE ON ICE

"Do you believe in miracles? Yes!" television announcer Al Michaels shouts frantically into the microphone over the roar of the crowd. He is witnessing one of the greatest upsets in Olympic history. A ragtag collection of college students from the United States is beating a heavily favored, professional Soviet team 4–3 in the Olympic ice hockey semifinals of the 1980 Winter Olympics, in Lake Placid, New York.

Old rivals

Before the upset, the Soviet team had dominated the sport, winning gold at the past four Olympic games. Team USA was a group of amateur hockey players who had never played together before training had begun. But this was only part of the story. In the years leading up to the game, the United States and **Soviet Union** were locked in a decades-long political conflict called the **Cold War**. This tension would set the stage for an international showdown.

"Nine out of ten times we play this team, they would beat us. But not tonight. Because tonight is our night. Tonight we win."

– Herb Brooks, Team USA coach

Tension rises

On the ice, Team USA battled with the skilled Soviets, keeping the game close. However, the United States was trailing at the end of the second period, 3–2. Early in the third period, the United States had managed to tie the game 3–3. The crowd was buzzing, chanting, and cheering the underdog team on. Only moments later, Mike Eruzione scored the go-ahead goal for the United States.

As the Soviets counterattacked, goaltender Jim Craig denied everything fired at him until the final horn had sounded. The crowd erupted as gloves and equipment were thrown in the air and the jubilant victors piled on each other in celebration. Team USA had won, leading the game to be known as the Miracle on Ice!

AN INTERNATIONAL SPORT

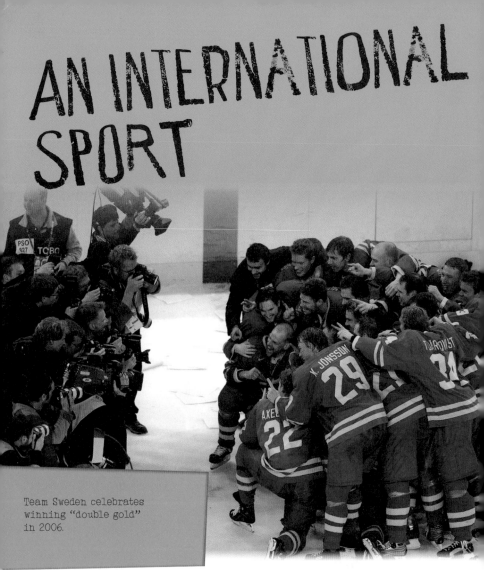

Team Sweden celebrates winning "double gold" in 2006.

While the 1980 Winter Olympics showcased two powerhouse hockey nations, hockey as an international sport has been around for over 100 years. Other triumphant moments have come from countries such as Sweden winning both the Olympics and International Ice Hockey Federation World Championship in 2006. Canada has won gold in the Olympics a record eight times. Other European countries such as Germany, Finland, and the Czech Republic also have a rich history in the world of hockey.

Hockey's popularity continues to grow internationally. And as this book will illustrate in the following pages, hockey's fast paced, hard-hitting action makes it the coolest sport on ice!

Goaltender Jim Craig of the U.S. Olympic team led his team to Olympic gold in 1980.

JIM CRAIG

Born: May 31, 1957, in North Easton, Massachusetts

Jim Craig was the 23-year-old goaltender for Team USA in the 1980 Winter Olympics. Craig started playing hockey when he was seven years old. He later went on to play college hockey, winning a championship at Boston College. From there, he was selected to be the goaltender for the U.S. Olympic team. He finished his hockey career playing in the National Hockey League.

NO WAY!

In 2012, Miracle On Ice defenseman Ken Morrow's game-worn USA jersey sold for $104,328! In 2010, teammate Mark Wells auctioned off his Olympic gold medal for a staggering $310,000!

A HISTORY OF ICE HOCKEY

While it is hard to pinpoint exactly when ice hockey started, it is believed that it has its origins in the British and Irish field games that involved sticks and balls. **Bandy**, shinty, and field hockey (or just "hockey") are sports that most closely resemble the game of ice hockey.

During colonial times, British soldiers posted in Canada took those games with them. Over time, people began to use frozen ponds, lakes, or rivers as clean, somewhat flat surfaces to play on. Players fashioned ice skates made of wood or bone (later metal), while the rubber ball was eventually replaced with a **puck** made of wood or rubber. Ice skating and ice hockey became so popular throughout the region that the first indoor ice rink was built in Montreal in 1862.

Ice hockey gained popularity all over the world. Here, hockey players are enjoying a brisk outdoor game in France around 1900.

SOCIETE D'EMBELLISSEMENT PATINAGE

Organized leagues

Local teams and leagues began to form throughout Canada and eastern parts of the United States. With the new leagues, rules of the game were established in the late 1800s. The governor general of Canada, Lord Stanley of Preston, introduced a championship trophy in 1892: the Stanley Cup (see page 11). The first of its kind, it instantly became the most prized trophy in the sport.

These are gold, silver, and bronze medals from the 2010 Winter Olympics in Vancouver. From a field of 12, only three take home a medal.

A truly international sport

Around the turn of the century, the sport made its way to Europe. Ice hockey was recognized as an Olympic sport at the 1920 Olympics in Antwerp, Belgium.

While the Stanley Cup is the most coveted trophy in the National Hockey League (NHL) (see page 10), the international game has its own prized awards: Olympic gold medals and the International Ice Hockey Federation (IIHF) World Championship. Teams come from every corner of the world. Australia, China, Mexico, and South Africa are just a few countries that participate in the international quest for gold!

GOING PROFESSIONAL

In its beginning, organized ice hockey was a popular sport for college and amateur players to participate in. As the sport's popularity rose, it became a spectator sport. People began paying money to watch the matches. Professional leagues formed, and players began to get paid for playing hockey. The most notable professional ice hockey organization is the National Hockey League (NHL).

Founded in 1917, the NHL began with five professional teams and later expanded to ten. However, by 1942, economic decline and World War II had reduced the NHL to just six teams: Montreal, Toronto, Boston, Detroit, Chicago, and New York, known as the *original six*. The original six era lasted from 1942 until 1967.

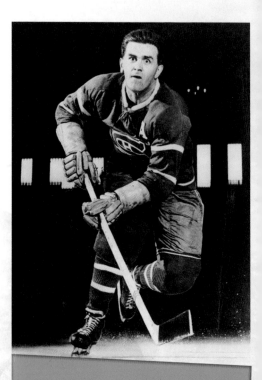

Maurice Richard (see page 12) was the driving force of the Montreal Canadiens during the "original six" era. Montreal won the Stanley Cup 10 times during the period—more than any other team. With 24 championship wins, it remains the most successful team in NHL history.

The NHL now

In 1967, the NHL expanded, adding additional clubs to the league. Currently, the NHL has 30 teams based in North America. NHL teams are made up of the top players from all over the world. Other countries, such as Russia, Sweden, Germany, and the United Kingdom, also have professional and semiprofessional ice hockey leagues.

THE STANLEY CUP

The Stanley Cup is still hockey's greatest award. Each season, the cup goes to the championship team from the NHL. All players' names from the winning teams are engraved on one of the rings at the base of the cup. To make room for new names, the oldest ring is removed and kept on display at the Hockey Hall of Fame in Toronto, Canada.

LEGENDS OF THE GAME

Every sport has its legends—the players who, over time, are still considered the greatest. These are some of the greatest to have ever put on skates and played the game.

Maurice "Rocket" Richard

August 4, 1921–May 27, 2000

Position: *Right wing, Montreal Canadiens*
Maurice Richard scored 30 or more goals in a season nine times in his career. He was also the first player to score 50 goals in 50 games during the 1944–45 season. Since 1999, the NHL has awarded the Maurice Richard Trophy to the league's regular season top scorer.

Gordie Howe

March 31, 1928–

Position: *Right wing, Detroit Red Wings*
Known as "Mr. Hockey," Gordie Howe played for the Detroit Red Wings for 26 seasons (1,767 games), in a career that spanned five decades. Howe was the NHL **MVP** (Most Valuable Player) six times and scored 801 goals in his career. Howe struck a balance between graceful scoring and punishing toughness.

Bobby Orr

March 20, 1948–

Position: *Defenseman, Boston Bruins*
Known as the greatest defenseman of his era, Bobby
Orr revolutionized hockey by becoming a **defensive**
player who made **offensive** plays and scored goals.
One season, he managed to score 46 goals and have
102 **assists**. Orr appeared in seven All-Star games.

NAIL-BITING MOMENT!

May 10, 1970

Simply known as "The Goal," Bobby Orr's goal in the 1970 NHL
playoffs versus the St. Louis Blues is the sport's most **iconic**
moment. Tied with three goals each early in **overtime**, Orr
received a pass from his teammate just in front of the net. As
he glided across the crease (see page 18), he took a driving shot
on goal and got tripped, sending him flying through the air. The
puck hit the back of the net, Orr landed, and the Boston Bruins
won the Stanley Cup.

Wayne Gretzky

January 26, 1961–

Position: *Center, Edmonton Oilers*
Known as "The Great One,"
Wayne Gretzky was the
complete hockey player. Gretzky
is the NHL's all-time leading
scorer, with an amazing 894
career goals. In the 1981–82
season, he set the record for
most goals scored in a season
with an astounding 92. When his
career ended in 1999, the NHL
retired his number (99) so that it
will never be worn again.

Jaromir Jagr

February 15, 1972–

Position: *Right wing, Pittsburgh Penguins*
One of the greatest players in the world, Jaromir Jagr leads the NHL
in scoring, assists, and points among European players. Known as an
explosive scorer and offensive threat, the Czechoslovakian has won the
Ice Hockey World championship, a gold medal, and the Stanley Cup. He
has appeared in the NHL All-Star game nine times.

Vladislav Tretiak

April 25, 1952–

Position: *Goaltender, Russian national team*

Consistently on "top players of all-time" lists, the Russian goaltender never played in the NHL. He led the Russian national team to 10 World Championships and three Olympic gold medals. Tretiak was the first Russian player to be inducted into the Hockey Hall of Fame.

NO WAY!

Hockey players are known for their clever, sometimes corny, nicknames. Can you tell which of these names belong to hockey players and which belong to professional wrestlers?

1. Nikolai "The Bulin Wall" Khabibulin
2. Dave "The Hammer" Shultz
3. Dwayne "The Rock" Johnson
4. Curtis "Cujo" Joseph
5. Randy "Macho Man" Savage

Answers:
1. Hockey; 2. Hockey;
3. Wrestler; 4. Hockey;
5. Wrestler

"You miss 100% of the shots you never take."

– *Wayne Gretzky*

GAME ON!

Now that we have an idea about the game's history and some of its best players, how do you play this game? Here are the basics.

No Way!

A Zamboni machine
Early on, people used shovels or scrapers to clear off and resurface ice. It could take four workers up to an hour to make the surface clean. Today, thanks to inventor Frank J. Zamboni's resurfacing machine, it is a one-person job that takes only about 10 minutes to complete!

Ice

Ice hockey can be played on any frozen surface—including frozen lakes or ponds in really cold areas! But if you are going to play organized hockey, you are going to need a rink designed for ice hockey.

Line markings

At an ice rink, the ice has lines just under the surface to mark the playing area. The ice surface is surrounded by a wall called the boards and protective glass (to keep the puck from entering the crowd). The rink is divided in half, with a red line at center ice. Each side has a blue line that marks each team's **defensive** or **attacking zone**. The area between the two blue lines is called the **neutral zone**.

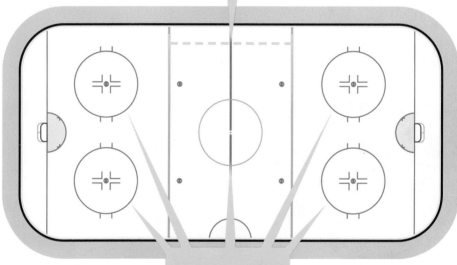

neutral zone

face-off circles

There are five face-off circles on the ice: two toward each end and one at center ice. These circles are where players line up to take face-offs whenever the play is whistled "dead" by a referee. Each end has a goal cage with a net attached to the back of it. The goal rests on **stanchions**, or upright bars, designed to allow the hard pipes some give if a player goes flying into them.

The goal

The goal mouth also has a line between the pipes that the puck needs to cross to count as a goal. In front of the net, there is a half circle that marks the goal crease (the area in which a goalie cannot be touched, unless someone gets pushed into him or her). Both teams have benches for players and coaches and a **penalty box** along the same side of the rink.

NO WAY!

At the 2002 Winter Games in Salt Lake City, Utah, the Canadian ice-making team embedded a Loonie (a gold-colored Canadian one-dollar coin) at center ice for good luck. After the men's and women's Canadian hockey teams both won gold, Wayne Gretzky dug the coin out of the ice and presented it to the hockey Hall of Fame.

Gear

Hockey players use a lot more equipment than in other sports. The average hockey player's equipment weighs about 12 pounds (5.5 kilograms). And don't forget an extra-large duffle bag to put it all in!

Skates

The fastest and slickest way to move on ice, skates also protect ankles and feet from flying pucks and other players' skate blades. Unlike normal ice skates, modern hockey skates are made from plastic, nylon, and materials such as **Kevlar** for maximum protection. The metal blade's edge attached at the bottom is not actually flat. Instead, it is a hollow half-moon shape that makes both edges of the skate a blade. Skate blades need to be sharpened regularly to keep them fast and responsive.

Pads

Have you ever fallen on ice? It hurts! Have you ever been crushed against the boards from a **body check** fighting for a puck? It's painful! Hockey players wear lots of pads to protect their bodies. Gloves, shoulder pads, elbow pads, neck guards, wrist guards, and shin guards are all part of a uniform.

Helmets

It is hard to believe, but up until 1979, players in the NHL were not required to wear helmets. Helmets are padded inside to protect the head and have a chin strap to hold them on during play. Players can choose to wear a visor that attaches to the helmet to protect their eyes. The rules for international play require that a protective visor is worn on all helmets, while youth hockey leagues require that the entire face is protected by a cage.

Zach Parise of the New Jersey Devils demonstrates the importance of protective pads as he falls to the ice during Game 5 of the 2012 NHL Stanley Cup Final in Newark, New Jersey.

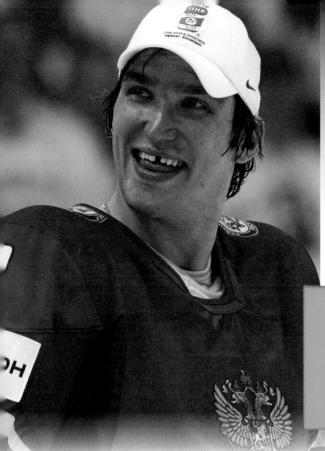

NO WAY!

With sticks, pucks, elbows, and skates all flying through the air, a hockey player's teeth don't always stay in. Tooth injuries are so common in hockey that every professional team has a dentist on-site for emergencies during the game. Players today wear custom mouth guards, but those don't always work!

Hockey superstar Alexander Ovechkin is well known for his missing front tooth. He lost it when he was high-sticked in the mouth in a game against the Atlanta Thrashers.

Sticks

In the early days, hockey sticks were made from one solid piece of wood and had a flat blade at the end at about a 45-degree angle. Modern sticks are made of carbon fiber, aluminum, or fiberglass and have curved blades. The new materials make the sticks lighter, stronger, and give the sticks better "feel." Sticks come in all sorts of lengths, colors, and materials. They can also come with a hefty price tag; some new sticks can cost over $300!

Players wrap their sticks with tape—but why? Because a stick without tape is smooth and slippery. Tape wrapped around the blade gives some padding, while tape around the shaft gives a better grip. A "knob" of tape at the top end of the shaft prevents the stick from sliding through gloves and makes it easier to pick up off the ice when dropped.

Goalie gear

Because the job of goalies is to keep the puck out of the net, they need special equipment (and ice in their veins) to stop frozen pucks from injuring them. First, goalies have oversized pads that are strapped to their legs to help them block shots. Goalies also wear a blocker—a flat, rectangular pad on the forearm of their stick hand. On the other side, they wear a leather catch glove, similar to a baseball mitt, to catch pucks. Goalies also have wider sticks that help with shot-blocking. Goalies' helmets have a built-in mask and cage to protect the face. The old goalie masks could look pretty scary!

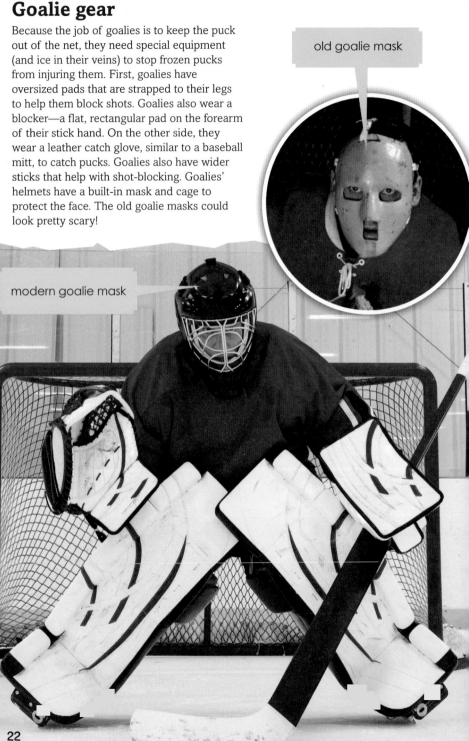

old goalie mask

modern goalie mask

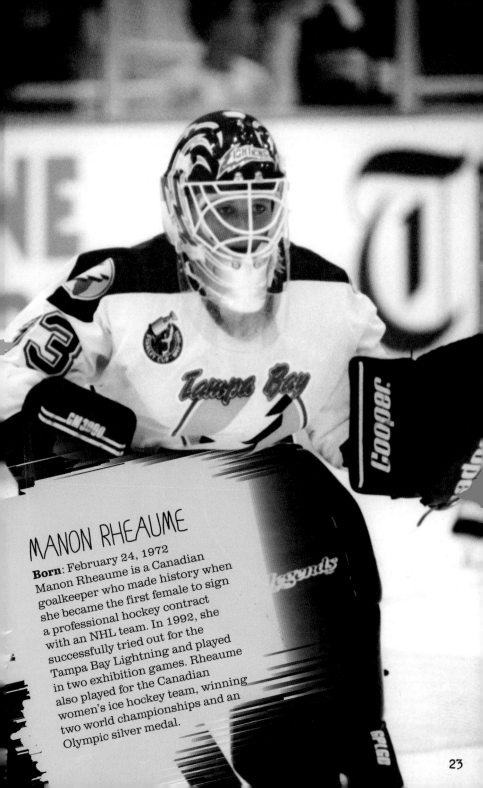

MANON RHEAUME

Born: February 24, 1972

Manon Rheaume is a Canadian goalkeeper who made history when she became the first female to sign a professional hockey contract with an NHL team. In 1992, she successfully tried out for the Tampa Bay Lightning and played in two exhibition games. Rheaume also played for the Canadian women's ice hockey team, winning two world championships and an Olympic silver medal.

DROP THE PUCK!

The object of hockey is the same as many other sports like soccer: to score by putting the playing object—in this case, the puck—in the goal.

Hockey pucks

Originally, rubber balls were used to play hockey. The puck, which is basically a ball with the top and bottom cut off to produce a disc shape, bounces less and stays closer to the ice. Pucks are frozen before games, which makes them even less bouncy. The side of the puck has a diamond-shaped texture for better grip and control.

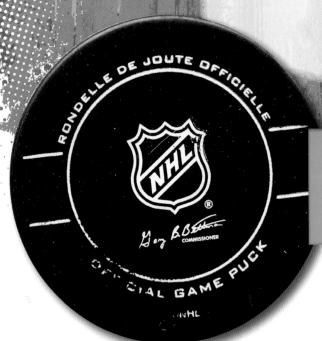

RONDELLE DE JOUTE OFFICIELLE

NHL

Gary B. Bettman
COMMISSIONER

OFFICIAL GAME PUCK

NHL

Regulation pucks are 3 inches (7.6 cm) wide, 1 inch (2.5 cm) thick, and weigh 6 ounces (170 grams).

"A puck is a hard rubber disc that hockey players strike when they can't hit one another."

– Jimmy Cannon, sports journalist

Shootouts and substitutions

A hockey game is made up of three periods lasting 20 minutes each, with two intermissions, or breaks, of 15 minutes. If the score is tied after 60 minutes of play, a "**sudden death**" overtime period of 20 minutes begins. This means the first team to score wins. If the score is still tied after overtime, it gets settled by a **shootout**. In NHL matches, this means three players on the team each get a shot at the goal. After these shots, the team with the most goals is awarded the victory. If the score is still tied, the shootout then goes to "sudden death," where each team gets a turn to have a shot at goal, and the winner is the first team to score while the other misses.

Teams usually have enough players to have four **lines** who can be substituted for other players during the game. Hockey can be tiring, so players play in short shifts, usually around 45 seconds at a time.

25

PLAYER POSITIONS

Each team has six players on the ice at a time:

Center. The offensive leader, the center mostly plays in the center area of the ice. A center is a playmaker and should be a good passer and have a great shot.

Right/Left wing: **Wingers** are players who are responsible for the offensive attack on either the right or left side of the ice. These players also have to fight along the boards to keep control of the puck on an offensive attack.

Right/Left defensemen: Two tough players assigned to each side of the ice, the defensemen's job is to stop the other team from taking shots. Defensemen also make passes to clear their zone and **breakout** up the ice. Defensemen can join their teammates for an offensive rush but usually hang around the **high slot** (area between the face-off circles near the blue line) to play defense if the puck is turned over to the other team.

Goalkeeper: The last line of defense, a goalkeeper stays in the crease in front of the net to block shots, communicate, and direct plays.

New Jersey Devils' goalkeeper Martin Brodeur blocks a shot from the Philadelphia Flyers' right winger Jakub Voracek.

JEROME IGINLA

Born: July 1, 1977

Jerome Iginla is a hugely talented hockey superstar. However, he is also known for being his generation's trailblazer for players of African descent. In a sport that has an abundance of players of European descent, "Iggy" has become one of the league's premiere physical and offensive threats. He is one of only 77 NHL players to have reached the 1,000-point (goals and assists) mark and has won two Olympic gold medals for Team Canada.

PASSING AND SHOOTING

Hockey players are very skilled at quickly skating forward, backward, or stopping. The better players can skate, the better they can increase their control and ability to make plays. They use a combination of skating and **stickhandling** to control the puck, pass it, and shoot it.

Passing

Passing the puck from one teammate to another is an important team skill. If players can make a great pass, they can make a great play. Assists (passes made by one player to a teammate who then scores) are almost as important as goals. Both goals and assists are recorded in hockey **statistics**.

The following are some of the main types of passes:

Cross-ice pass: A pass where the puck goes from one side of the ice to the other

Backhand pass: A pass made using the backside of the stick blade

Drop pass: A pass a player pushes behind him or her to another teammate while both travel forward

Saucer pass: A pass that gets elevated off the ice to fly over opposing players' sticks

No-look pass: A pass made by a player who doesn't look where he or she is passing but knows a player will be in position to receive it

Dallas Stars player Michael Ryder makes a saucer pass over the stick of the Edmonton Oilers' Ladislav Smid.

Shooting

Shooting is the most exciting part of the game. There are a number of ways to put the puck in the net. A slap shot is when a player cocks the stick to **wind up** (swing back) and let it rip. A wrist shot is a shot where the shooter flicks or snaps his or her wrist without first winding up. A shovel shot is simply pushing the puck forward toward the goal.

Seth Griffith fires a wrist shot past Oscar Dansk in a junior hockey game in London, Canada.

"If you want money, go to the bank. If you want bread, go to the bakery. If you want goals, go to the net."

– Brooks Laich, Washington Capitals center

Special shots

A backhand shot means the puck is launched from the back of the stick's blade instead of the front. A tip is when a player redirects another player's shot by positioning the stick to deflect, or change, its position.

A **deke** (short for "decoy") is when a player tries to misdirect a defenseman or goalie by faking a pass or shot. While skating, passing, stickhandling, and shooting are the most important skills to learn, players also need to be able to do all these within the rules of the game.

FIVE FOR FIGHTING!

The old joke goes: I went to a fight the other night and a hockey game broke out! Due to the physical nature of the game, players often get into scuffles that sometimes result in fights. As the rules of the game have changed over time to prevent them, fights occur less and less. A fight in today's game will incur a **major penalty,** earning a player five minutes in the penalty box—a big price to pay for not keeping a cool head.

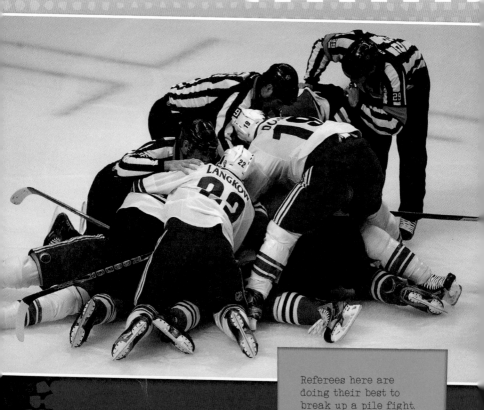

Referees here are doing their best to break up a pile fight.

Referees and rules

Just like any other sport, hockey has its own set of rules to play by. The people who enforce these rules are called referees and linesmen. Games will have two referees and two linesmen in charge of the game. The referees are responsible for the overall supervision of the game, while linesmen are responsible for calling line infractions, or rule-breaking (for example, icing and offsides; see below).

Both NHL and the international game have a ton of rules—too many to list here! Here are the most important rules to remember:

Offsides: Players are not allowed to enter their attack zone before the puck does. Breaking this rule results in a stoppage of play and a face-off in the neutral zone.

Icing: To avoid wasting time, you cannot just shoot the puck all the way down the ice. However, if your team or the opposing goalie touches the iced puck first, play will continue.

Hooking: A hook is when a player uses a stick to hold another player back from reaching the puck.

Holding: A player cannot restrain, or hold back, another player by grabbing onto him or her.

Slashing: A slash is when a player forcefully uses a stick like a weapon to hit another player's stick or body.

Tripping: Players are not allowed to use sticks, legs, feet, or arms to trip an opponent.

Boarding: Skaters are not allowed to body check an opponent from behind into the boards.

Highsticking: Players need to keep their sticks below their shoulders.

When players break the rules, they have to spend time in the penalty box (see page 33).

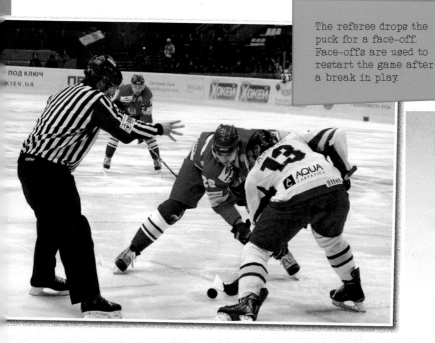

The referee drops the puck for a face-off. Face-offs are used to restart the game after a break in play.

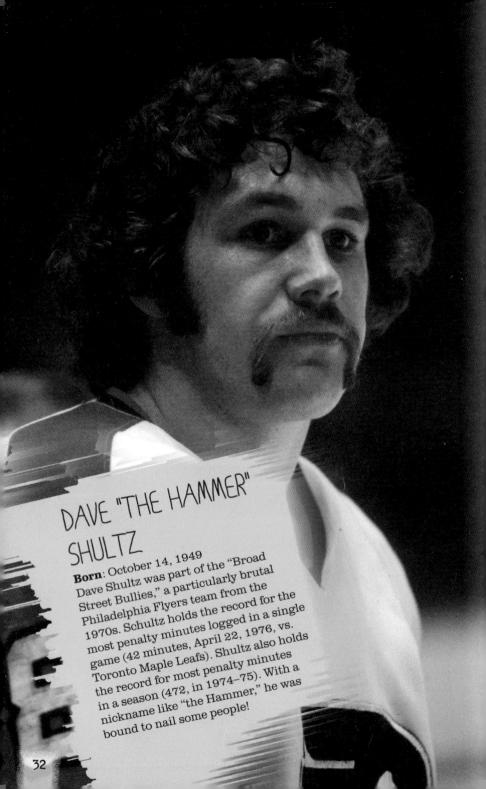

DAVE "THE HAMMER" SHULTZ

Born: October 14, 1949

Dave Shultz was part of the "Broad Street Bullies," a particularly brutal Philadelphia Flyers team from the 1970s. Schultz holds the record for the most penalty minutes logged in a single game (42 minutes, April 22, 1976, vs. Toronto Maple Leafs). Shultz also holds the record for most penalty minutes in a season (472, in 1974–75). With a nickname like "the Hammer," he was bound to nail some people!

Penalties

A **minor penalty** will put the player in the box for two minutes, thereby giving the opposing team a power play. A power play gives one team an advantage, because it has five skaters on the ice (not including the goalie) compared to the other team's four. Teams can have up to two players in the box at a time.

Goalies are always in the game— if a goalie gets called for a penalty, one of the other five players serves the time for him or her. Sometimes both teams will be called for penalties at the same time (called coincidental penalties), making the game four-on-four for two minutes. If a player is interfered with on a quality scoring chance, the puck carrier will be awarded a penalty shot.

Only the shooter and the goaltender are in play for a penalty shot.

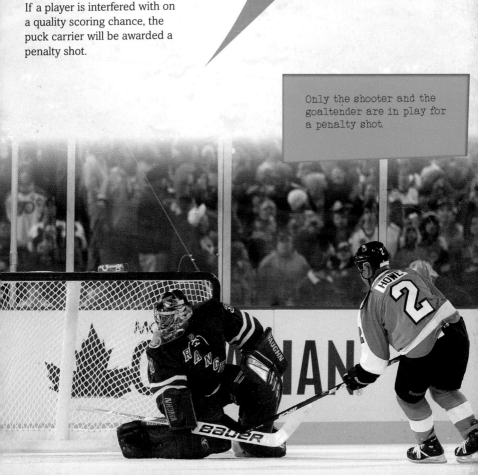

HOCKEY IS FOR EVERYONE

Referees keep hockey games fair by enforcing the rules. But if we want to play fair, we need to let anybody who wants to play participate. It is important to remember that hockey is just a game and can be enjoyed by all.

Youth leagues

Most countries with international hockey teams have youth programs for boys and girls that teach the basic skills and encourage sportsmanship and teamwork, in addition to promoting an active lifestyle. Leagues have age bracket divisions with corresponding labels such as *mite*, *squirt*, and *bantam*. Recreational youth teams are organized for fun, but they do hold tournaments and championships.

National under-20 hockey teams compete every year in the World Junior Hockey Championship.

Junior hockey

Junior hockey teams are for more skilled players between the ages of 16 and 20. Much more competitive than youth leagues, the juniors game is like the amateur game in terms of speed and ability. Junior teams compete internationally for the IIHF World Juniors Championship, in addition to the Youth Olympics. High Schools throughout over 40 U.S. states have squads that participate in interscholastic competition.

Sled hockey is fast-paced and highly physical, just like ice hockey. It has become a very popular Paralympic sport.

SLED HOCKEY

Sled hockey (known as sledge hockey internationally) was invented in Stockholm, Sweden, in the 1960s. Designed to allow players with physical disabilities to play hockey, it is played on a customized sled that has skate blades underneath it. Players propel themselves with their arms and use two shortened hockey sticks. The basic rules of ice hockey apply. Sled hockey can also be played by individuals who do not have a disability. Sled hockey didn't become an official event until the Lillehammer 1994 Paralympic Winter Games.

35

College hockey

Popular among both male and female student athletes from the beginning of the 20th century, college hockey is still an exciting and competitive arena in the United States and Canada. Colleges are increasingly becoming the resource for the NHL. In 2010, almost 29 percent of the active players had played college hockey.

RYAN NUGENT-HOPKINS

Born: April 12, 1993
Center, Team Canada
Ryan Nugent-Hopkins was born in Burnaby, British Columbia, Canada. One of today's most explosive young talents in the NHL, he will also play center for Team Canada in the 2014 Sochi Winter Olympics. During his **rookie** season for the Edmonton Oilers in 2011, he scored 18 goals and had 34 assists. Not bad for an 18-year-old!

Women's ice hockey

It took a while, but women's ice hockey finally made its Olympic debut at the 1998 Winter Olympics in Nagano, Japan. While the popularity of the women's game has grown in other countries, Canada and the United States have dominated the sport. Since its Olympic introduction, Canada has won three gold medals (2002, 2006, 2010), while the United States has taken home one (1998). Women's international game play shares most of the men's rules, but the IIHF does not allow body checking in the women's game.

The United States women's team beat China 12–1 on their way to Olympic silver in 2010.

Hockey around the world

Apart from the "big seven" (Canada, the United States, Czech Republic, Sweden, Finland, Russia, and Slovakia), over 50 other countries have ice hockey programs in development. Depending on where they are from and how they learned to play, players have different styles of play. North American players tend to play a more physical brand of hockey, while Europeans stress the finesse and speed of the game.

AIMING TO BE THE BEST

The greatest players in hockey come from all over the world to represent their countries at the Olympics. Some of them are professionals and some are amateurs. But they all have one goal: being the best in the world. Here are some of the top players who are likely to be representing their countries at the 2014 Winter Olympics, to be held in Sochi in Russia.

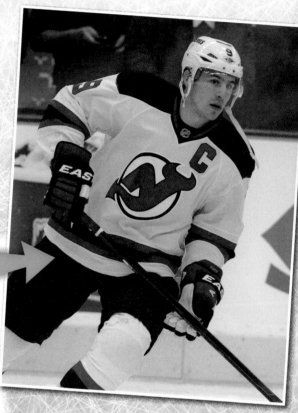

Zach Parise (United States)

Zach Parise makes plays happen fast. As the alternate captain on Team USA, he helped lead the team to a silver medal in the 2010 Winter Olympics. In the same year, he was named to the Olympic All-Star team. He scored over 30 goals in the NHL for four seasons in a row between 2006 and 2010.

Jordan Eberle (Canada)

Jordan Eberle is a dynamic right winger for the Edmonton Oilers of the NHL. Before turning professional, Eberle managed to win gold in the 2009 World Junior Championships for Canada. In the 2011–12 NHL season, he scored 34 goals and had 42 assists, and he was selected for the NHL All-Star game.

Mikko Koivu (Finland)

Mikko Koivu is the captain of both the Minnesota Wild and the Finnish national team. He led the Finns to a gold medal in the 2011 IIHF Men's World Championship.

Henrik Zetterberg (Sweden)

One of the game's best two-way players (a **forward** who plays defense as well as offense), Zetterberg is a leader on and off the ice. As a Detroit Red Wing, he won the Conn Smythe Trophy in 2008 for the MVP in the NHL playoffs. He has been a member of Team Sweden since 2001 and won gold at the 2006 Winter Olympics.

NAIL-BITING MOMENT!
SWEDISH GOLD

In 1994, the pressure was on Sweden to win its first-ever Olympic gold in Lillehammer, Norway. With less than two minutes left to play of the gold medal match, with Canada leading 2–1 until then, Magnuss Svennson scored to tie the game. In overtime, the teams remained deadlocked at two goals each. In the shootout, Sweden's Peter Forsberg outwitted Canadian goalkeeper Cory Hirsch with a nasty deke (decoy) and stuffed it in the net. Canada missed on its turn, giving Sweden its first Olympic gold. This was a moment so glorious that Sweden commemorated Forsberg's deke on a postage stamp!

HOW TO GET SKATING

Now that we know a lot about hockey, how do we get playing?

Learning how to skate

The best way to learn how to ice skate is to work on the basics: balance, skating forward, skating backward, turning, and stopping. Make sure you are wearing pads and a helmet, because you are going to be falling a lot! As you improve, you can try more advanced skills like the hockey stop, increasing your speed, and skating with your stick.

A lot of places have recreation ice rinks that are open to the public. If there isn't one where you live, check neighboring towns. If you live somewhere with a cold winter, you shouldn't have any problem finding an outside rink to skate on!

WARNING!

If it gets really cold and lakes or rivers freeze, you might think it's safe to skate on them. However, it is very important that you only skate at proper ice rinks. Ice may look like it is strong enough to hold you, but it is often not the same thickness all over. Accidents can happen when people play on thin ice.

Skating? But it's summer!

Remember that hockey skills can be practiced without ice. Street hockey is a simpler version of ice hockey that you can play when you are ice-challenged. Most sporting goods stores sell the equipment designed for street hockey, including skates. But all you really need is a stick, a ball, and a net. So lace up those shoes and hit the sidewalk!

TALK THE TALK!

Even if you don't look so hot on your skates, you can impress your friends by using some of this fancy hockey lingo.

Biscuit: The puck

Between the pipes: Into the net

Brain bucket: A helmet

Enforcer: An aggressive player who protects the more skilled members of his or her team

Five hole: The space between the goalie's legs

Hat trick: Three goals in one game

Light the lamp: Score a goal

Sin bin: The penalty box

Stripes: Referee

Top shelf: Scoring a goal under the **crossbar**, hitting the top of the net

These teenagers are enjoying a game of street hockey in Paris, France.

41

QUIZ

How much of an ice hockey fanatic are you?
Test your ice hockey knowledge with this quiz.

1. Every year, the NHL presents the _____ to its championship team.

a) Lady Byng Memorial Trophy
b) FA Cup
c) Mallo Cup
d) Stanley Cup

2. He is known as "The Great One." Who is he?

a) Mario Lemieux
b) Justin Bieber
c) Wayne Gretzky
d) none of the above

3. The area of ice between the two blue lines is called:

a) neutral zone
b) reverse zone
c) no go zone
d) defensive zone

4. A hockey game has this many periods:

a) 4
b) 5
c) 2
d) 3

5. A pass that rises off the ice surface is called a:

a) drop pass
b) bad pass
c) tape-to-tape pass
d) saucer pass

6. The referees who watch for line violations are called:

a) official timekeepers
b) Bob and Doug
c) linesmen
d) call them anything you want, just don't let them hear you

7. The first time and place ice hockey was played at the Olympics was:

a) Haagen-Dazs, Denmark, 1926
b) Antwerp, Belgium, 1920
c) Lake Placid, New York, 1980
d) Lillehammer, Norway, 1994

8. The penalty for fighting is:

a) 10 minutes
b) 5 minutes
c) no video games for a week
d) 2 minutes

7–8 correct answers: Clearly, you know your stuff when it comes to ice hockey! Perhaps you could be competing for medals in the future.

4–6 correct answers: Not bad. Try to join a club in your area and get some practice in.

1–3 correct answers: There is so much to learn about ice hockey. Try to watch some on television or on the Internet, and see if you can learn more about it. You might find you want to play!

Answers

1. d
2. c
3. a
4. d
5. d
6. c
7. b
8. b

GLOSSARY

assist pass that leads to a score

attacking zone area that your team attacks in, closer to the opposition's goal than to your own

bandy sport played on ice that is similar to ice hockey

body check using the body to hit players against the boards, to the ice, or off the puck

breakout play to get the puck out of the defending team's zone

Cold War period between 1947 and 1990 during which an intense political and military escalation developed between the United States and Russia without actually leading to war

crossbar horizontal bar that connects the goalposts

defensive playing on the defense

defensive zone area that your own team defends

deke short for "decoy," a fake or false movement used by the puck-handler to trick a defending player

forward another name for the front three offensive players (center, left wing, right wing)

high slot area between the face-off circles near the blue line

iconic famous or most well known

Kevlar trademarked name for very strong synthetic material

line group of three forwards who play together in a game. A line consists of a left wing, a center, and a right wing.

major penalty penalty that is five minutes long

minor penalty two-minute penalty

MVP most valuable player

neutral zone area of the ice between the blue lines

offensive playing on the attack

overtime additional period of five minutes that takes place when a game ends in a tie after three periods of play. Overtime periods follow the sudden death format.

penalty box self-contained area where players sit to serve penalty minutes

puck black disc made of hard rubber that is used as a ball

rookie first-year player in a sports team

Soviet Union former country that included Russia and many smaller nations from Asia and Eastern Europe. The Soviet Union broke up in 1991.

shootout one-on-one shooting contest to decide the winner of the game if it is tied after

stanchion upright flexible tube used to keep the goal in place on the ice

statistic piece of numerical data

stickhandling using the hockey stick to control and move the puck

sudden death (also known as sudden victory) period in overtime in which the first team to score wins the game

wind up when a player swings back the hockey stick behind him or her before hitting the puck

winger slang for the left wing or right wing positions

FIND OUT MORE

Books

Gitlin, Martin. *The Stanley Cup: All About Pro Hockey's Biggest Event* (Winner Takes All). Mankato, Minn.: Capstone, 2013.

Johnson, Tami. *Girls' Ice Hockey: Dominating the Rink* (Snap Books: Girls Got Game). Mankato, Minn.: Capstone, 2008.

Latimer, Clay. *VIP Pass to a Pro Hockey Game Day: From the Locker Room to the Press Box (and Everything in Between)* (Game Day). Mankato, Minn.: Capstone, 2011.

Sias, John. *Kids' Book Of Hockey: Skills, Strategies, Equipment, and the Rules of the Game.* New York: Citadel, 2000.

Web sites

www.hhof.com
This is the web site of the Hockey Hall Of Fame. It contains all you need to know about ice hockey, with information about honored players, Stanley Cup information, a photo gallery, and much more.

www.NHL.com
This is the official web site for the National Hockey League.

www.olympic.org/sochi-2014-winter-olympics
This is the official site for the 2014 Winter Olympics at Sochi, Russia. As the event approaches, you will be able to read about the players involved and any team news.

www.usahockey.com
This is the official web site of USA Hockey. It gives information about all aspects of hockey in the United States, from youth leagues to Team USA.

Places to visit

Hockey Hall Of Fame
30 Yonge Street
Toronto, Ontario, Canada M5E 1X8
www.hhof.com

U.S. Hockey Hall Of Fame Museum
801 Hat Trick Avenue
Eveleth, Minnesota 55734
www.ushockeyhall.com

INDEX